ABOUT THE AUTHOR

Anne has had an interesting life. After completing her education in Australia and the UK, she worked for many years for a pharmaceutical company in the US.

She retired to France with her husband and enjoyed life close to the mountains and the vineyards of the Languedoc Roussillon region.

She now calls Australia home and is still close to the mountains and the sea.

To the Poets of yesteryear, especially John Keats,
who have inspired me to write poetry.
I thank them.

Anne Hay

THE MISTS OF TIME

AUSTIN MACAULEY PUBLISHERS™

LONDON • CAMBRIDGE • NEW YORK • SHARJAH

A CIP catalogue record for this title is available from the British Library.

ISBN 9781528991810 (Paperback)
ISBN 9781528991827 (ePub e-book)

www.austinmacauley.com

First Published (2021)
Austin Macauley Publishers Ltd
25 Canada Square
Canary Wharf
London
E14 5LQ

POEMS

Notre Dame de Paris

It's Paris in the moonlight of yesteryear,
It's the magic and beauty of the old and ancient.
It's Notre Dame, the beautiful lady on the Seine,
Reaching upwards in heavenly glory.

Her lights went out when the fire caused her harm;
Then the people of Paris came and stood around,
Some cried, some sang hymns
As Notre Dame was burning that night, when all the world looked on.

In the early morning light, when we looked outside, we saw that
Notre Dame was hurt, and blackened, but still standing;
We prayed again that she would still be with us, and in our lives.
We prayed there, when we were passing.

We were in awe of her beauty and her stained-glass windows,
And we had hoped, during the night, that she would still be a vital part of
    Paris and our lives.

Notre Dame is Paris, and it would be sad
If she could not be saved, but a miracle took place;
Yes, her heart was saved, and she will live again.
Like Phoenix she will rise from the ashes, and give us
Comfort in her arms again. We need all of that to survive.

We will all stand watch as she is being repaired,
We will see the peoples' love of Paris, and their own Notre Dame;
Once more they can put their arms around the ancient church,
That is Paris itself, and watch over her until she is restored.

The magical stained-glass windows and vaulted ceilings
Have a mystical feeling as we walk through the door
Of a place where the world worships, and becomes
Haunted by the mystery of life and death.
Where time takes us back to the beginning of life.

Notre Dame is Our Mother,
She protects us in our hour of need.
She will always be there, to comfort and support
The down-trodden and the sad old tramps.

Many kings of France have been crowned inside;
Looking upwards they must have seen a better life,
And men of politics, have walked inside Notre Dame;
There they have known pride of place and were humbled.

There they think of their role in France's destiny
There, they listen and heed the scriptures.
Life is a test of knowing who you are, and
Helping your country through the hard times.
But, soon outside, they forget their fear, and then
They forget why they were there.

A Poet's Melancholy

Did Keats teach me how to write?
   Did I always feel this way?
I like to write and sometimes cannot stop;
   But write like Keats, and Shelly and Wordsworth
Their days have since past, and I
   Could never be as good.

They were lyrical and sensitive and
   Always understood, the need to tread softly;
Their tender words implied an overpowering ecstasy and
   Their words were ever-changing
The colours and the mood.

If only I could be as good, and get the feeling right,
   The deepest love and sadness of a love that couldn't be.
Yet, yearning for the ecstasy, and feeling pain beyond pain
   Of love that couldn't be.

Such sadness and such melancholy
   Could make a poet mad,
Because they bared their soul for the love
   They couldn't have.

Sometimes in the mists of time
   We take up pen and paper
To write about the days gone by,
   To write and bring the truth to light
Of love, of fearless thoughts and ideas;
   Of hopes and brighter days ahead.

What then, we say, what then?
    And scribble words with pen
The lines on paper say the words
    But we cannot hear them.
No, we have to hear the words, so speak
    Out loud and bring the words to life,
And then the melancholy of the day, will
    Turn to love at night.

The clear sounds of the running stream
    The moonlight on the dales,
The perfumed air in the morning glow,
    Gives the poet reason to live.
His melancholy surrounds him
    And once more he writes of love.

The brave kind of love, the weak kind of love
    He cannot escape its painful haunting;
He dreams of the glory of love
    And hopes that it is never ending.
But surely, there comes a day, when a poet
    Will write and say,
That true love can be forever, and that
    Love is worth the loving, and in this knowledge
We can endure anything, and make the world
    A better place.

What Time Is It?

Can we be sure that we will be on time,
As we hurry through our daily lives?
Can we be sure that the alarm will ring
If we get it right today, what will tomorrow bring?

Setting out on time to catch the bus or train
Will there be time enough, and is there a timetable there?
Thinking as we ride along, what next, then
Arriving at our destination with time to spare.

Time is something we cannot bottle
We exist, that's time, and then the morrow
Will show us how we spent the time
Of yesterday, when time was passing by.

Again, today is our time and our place,
We start anew with thoughts, but do we have the time to
Bank them, and save them for
Today, tonight, tomorrow?

The time is now, now is the time
Each second, minute, hour is precious
We cannot go back, the clock ticks on,
We hope today, will bring the morrow.

A better tomorrow means no sorrow
We have no time to grieve.
Can we at least, have a fleeting glance
Of the future and its place on earth?

For time can't be stilled, it can't be harnessed;
The only way to feel the touch of time
Is to use it best, so that twenty-four hours
Will turn into another day, another week, another year.

Then we can say, we still feel time,
We still tell time because
It's on our wrists, and every clock, tick-tock.
It's good to have time on our side,
For time and tide wait for no man
This is true we know; therefore
Time is of the essence.

As we go, to travel far and wide
On trains, and boats and planes
Up, up into the sky we go
Does time stand still in space?

So many light years away, they say
Where time is never ending.
But our time is measured best
With the chimes of old Big Ben
With its melodious ring,
We ask, what time is it?

If we do not look for, and find the time
We will be left behind,
So we must try to seize the day, in Latin, *carpe diem*,
Then contemplate our future, as time goes by.

A Beautiful World to Share with My Love

It's rather late, but better late than never
I felt the need to write a bit, to put my thoughts in words.
I'm all alone now, no husband anymore;
So I like to write a bit, I think it's good.

To write about my thoughts and sorrows,
The need to focus on the past, can bring sadness
But then I realise, it's best to feel the gladness
Of knowing my husband, the fun and the madness.

Together our adventures took us down rivers in kayaks and
Down the long ski slopes,
The world was ours, as we played in nature's wilderness,
We loved nature's big sky and her vast forests;
This beautiful world where we played and loved.

We camped and we hiked and we climbed to the top
Of any large mountain or hill top.
We could see the world spread out below
With the mists and the villages where we used to go.

We would walk through the trees, and high rocky crags
Down, and down we would walk to the next valley through the damp
  mossy glens.
Our path was up on high again, on the mountain ridge
Where eagles soared in the bright blue sky.

As we walked or skied or kayaked, we always
Felt the beauty of the moment of the great outdoors.
The fresh air, the bird songs, the wind in the trees;
The freedom we had in nature will always be with me,
We were lucky to know this beautiful world together.

Once more we sat around the campfire with friends
The night sky was dark but dotted with stars.
We could hear far, far away the distant call of
The coyote high in the mountain, first on one side, then the other.

They knew where we were, and so did the bear
But we stayed and delighted in nature's night air.
With a steak and beer and good friends for cheer
We camped on Ed's field under the big fir;
Out in the wilderness, under the stars,
A beautiful world to share with my love.

The Days You Loved Me

Do not forsake me when you need me the most,
Reach out your hand and I will take it in mine,
Our world is small, and beyond the gate there are
Mountains and hills and villages and sea,
Do not forsake me yet.

If I have caused you to wonder who I am
If I have not told you that I loved you,
It is because your heart took a different turn
And you showed coldness and distain;
But I don't know why, because I am who you loved
When we were young and you found me;
The days of dancing and rivers and Texas,
Were days of adventures and fun and friends.
The days you loved me.

So walk back to me and hold my hand
Let us dance and sing again;
We loved life so much and travelled far
We cannot leave it now.
Hold me close and remember our past
We can relive those precious day again.
Don't say goodbye just yet.
Let us drink a glass of wine,
And think on the days when we met.

Under the Big Texas Sky

Come dance with me near the river bank
With the moonlight kissing the water flow;
Come dance with me like we used to do
When the music was fast or the music was slow.

When we danced in our field of dreams,
That's where you asked me to marry you.
We had run the river in kayaks that day
And danced to Strauss waltzes that night.

A surprise it was, when you asked for my hand
Suddenly out of the blue,
What were you thinking, what brought this on?
The waltz, the moon, the river and you?

The green field was there in the Texas night
The music of Strauss echoed out,
And we danced and danced to our favourite waltz
Then you kissed me and called me sweetheart.

The great Texas moon shone high in the sky,
The stars were like diamonds so bright,
As we waltzed in our field under the wide-open sky
In love with each other that night.

An Ode to a Gentleman

In an English country garden,
    Surrounded by Mozart, Bach and others
And Family members too,
    This is where I see Tony now.
A beautiful man, a father and a friend.
    He'll never be too far away
Around us as we work and play.

One thinks about the conversations had
    About the fun and the sad,
But most of all, about his help
    And the times in which he felt
That he was needed and was there.
    He still will be right at your hand
To guide you as your lives expand, and move
    Towards a richer place,
One of peace and of grace.

All knew him as he walked on by
    His wonderful twinkle in the eye.
Even the young could see his beauty,
    His love of everyone and his duty.
He radiated a shining warmth that today is rare,
    His inspiration to all around made
His moments on this earth abound
    With so much love and care.

The music that he loved so much,
    He played for all to share.
In church he brought the hymns alive
    And song was everywhere.
His talent was so delicate and free,
    And he has given these gifts to you and me,
As we remember the music from his heart.

For Tony, music was the food of love.
 Each and everyone, be they family or friend
Will have a special tune that Tony played.
 And it will be forever etched
Upon their hearts and in their lives,
 And this will always keep his
Music and his love alive.

Gallipoli

During the night of April 25, 1915
    The Anzacs came ashore on the beach at Gallipoli.
The troops made their way up the beach, fighting for every inch.
    They knew they had to make the best of it, or die.
Their mate-ship is what helped them endure the worst hardships,
    Under constant attack with no shelter.

Each soldier was important to one and all;
    They became family, and helped each other through hell.
They were there, and comforted one another during the battles,
    In their rough sort of way;
They were together, and at each other's side when
    Their mates lay wounded and dying, they were there.

Who else could have been close enough to hold a hand,
    To dress a wound, to read a letter to a dying man?
Who else, could tell them they will be home soon, that the battle was nearly
    over?
    This was to comfort the soldier, his mate, who could have been himself.
They were mostly young boys who left their homes, looking for adventure.
    How sad, how tragic was this war, their lives were lost forever.

Soldiers have an inner strength, which they call upon
    And their mate-ship also helps to fight, the fight of their lives.
The Anzacs have a spirit rare, this is what is remembered by
    Countries they helped and fought their war, and won;
But at what cost, they won because they could not lose and give up
    The freedom of the world to something so dark and terrible.
They won, and fought to save humanity, their cost was great and legendary.

Their courage comes, we know not how,
    To fight to save their fellow men and comfort them to the end,
Is selfless and heroic, never thinking of themselves;
    Never shirking their duties and their team.
For all of this, the Anzacs will always be remembered by
    Countries near and far, by friends and relatives they left behind,
Not knowing what lay ahead, nothing could prepare them
    For the fields of the dying and the dead.

But red poppies sprung up from the terrible earth, as if they
    Were giving back, and giving birth to a new age, with no more war;
No more wars in a foreign place where men died alone, in distant fields, long
    ago.
The Anzacs will never be forgotten, we will always remember them.
They died for their country and their mates.
        They gave us what we have today, our freedom, and our lives.
                    LEST WE FORGET

The Norfolk Fishermen

The Norfolk sky is bold and beautiful,
    The windswept beach is wide and long,
The fishermen go out to sea and the storms are often strong;
    But coming home with the catch is worth a bob or two.

The boats are old, the sails are torn, the nets are broken too
    But they'll never complain, because you see
It's the life they want to live.
    The fishermen of the Norfolk coast come
Home in the morning, when the clouds are high;
    They clear the decks and clean them down and furl the nets and sails,
Until it's time to start again and go out in the storm and gales.

They won't give up, this is their life
    They may die at sea.
They know this, but are not afraid
    Perhaps like you or me.
But going down to the sea again
    They can't resist its call;
As the wind sweeps over the harbour walls
    They get their boats ready for the next great haul.
These fishermen of the Norfolk coast,
    Who have seen many a ghost,
On a windy night at sea.

England's Green and Pleasant Land

On walking along the hedge rows
When the dew is twinkling on the branch,
The Robin sings as the sun rises, over the distant hill.
I see the blackberries in the hedge shimmering there
And pick one, and eat it in the morning air.

I smell the morning as it awakes, this
England, this land that I love.
The grasses, all of different hue, with colour greens anew;
The flowing trees that close in, over the path that I take.
I am comforted when on my walk I see
The tall green grass under the meadow tree.

There, down in the valley, I see the cows ambling in for milking,
They are part of the tapestry of life in a slow and gentle time.
The farmers work so hard but their life is bountiful,
They are close to Mother Earth and are content.

Then passing by on market day, the village town is colourful,
I buy some lunch and sit beside the river, with the dappled
Sunlight making poetry, as I watch the happy
People on the village green, who love this place,
This England, as summer smiles upon them.

This earth, this England is still as gentle as it was
When Constable was painting the peaceful countryside.
It has not changed, and we must keep it so,
So our grandchildren will know, its beauty and its soul.

I'll keep on walking through the dales and hills,
Keep on feeling light of foot to know
That our countryside is looking as it should.
It is a glory to behold,
This England's green and pleasant land.

Love Is the Reason We Live

Love takes its toll,
It leaves behind our very soul,
It creates the tears we cry,
It creates the reasons why
We love, and dare to dream
Of hope, to keep the dream alive
That love will conquer all.

It makes us who we are
For better or for worse.
Love is part of us; without it
We cannot share our every care,
Without it we are empty.

I want to care again, and live
To share my love with someone
Who, like me, can see a future far away;
And together for companions' sake
We'll learn to grow, but then escape
To somewhere where we'll always love to be,
And find the world and its infinity.

Is love the reason why we get up every day?
Hoping that the day will bring
A purpose and a new-found friend;
A knowledge that in every word
We can help and be heard.
Our deeds will be forever good
If we love as we should;
And finding love, don't let it go.

Hold hands and walk along the shore
For romance is to be cherished
And once more, to love again
And to be sure, that each and every day
You will whisper your love to me,
Keeping romance alive and free
We'll walk hand in hand down to the sea.

And we will dance together all the time
For loving you will be just fine, if
Loving me will always be forever;
And we'll bring our hopes and dreams
Of everlasting love, into a world
That needs love more and more.

So holding hands, we'll walk along the beach
Being happy in our happiness and grateful
That we found each other, along the sandy shore
Of timelessness and waves and blue sky.
It is the place to fall in love again,
I wonder why.

Poems and Our Souls

All the poets of yesteryear were so expressive
    They found their voice in rhyme.
They walked through the glorious fields of daffodils
    And rowed across the wide-open lakes.
They had their eyes open, they looked around,
    They never took their eyes off nature,
For nature was all around.

This is why, now, we can see through their eyes
    The reason they wrote what they did.
The hills and the dales of Yorkshire were too stunning
    To never recall. The poets wrote about
England's green and pleasant land, so that we may
    Paint their pictures in our minds.

Because we have read their works, and walked upon the
    Ground they wrote about,
We know how precious their love of beauty was to them;
    They wrote so others could also
Feel the magic of the countryside they loved,
    And wanted future generations to share
The love, of where they had been, and what they had seen.
    This would leave its mark for eternity, to be discovered
By the young in love.

It opened up our eyes when we read their poems
    So beautiful were they, so rare.
How did they look upon this earth, with sadness and despair?
    They had their sorrows, and their loves
But the very beauty that they told was of the
    Beauty all around, it was theirs to weave
Into a poem, it was theirs to ponder in delight.

Yes, it was about lost love, and nymphs and glens in
    Green forest light, with ferns and moss
And timelessness. The poems sang to us and painted
    Endless visions of a poet's dreams and wishes.
They had found their voices, they had changed the world,
    And brought to us their thoughts to share,
And it is this, that gave us the beauty they found,
    As we read their wondrous works.

Can we ever contribute such elegance with pen and paper?
    We need love's pain to take us there,
Into their world and their despair, but writing, healed their
    Wounds and left us with their words, their fears,
And painted landscapes from the air, their visions
    Of the hedgerows and the fields, and on through
Deep forests and the weald, where once were tall and gracious trees.

We are blessed for having read, and understood what was said
    In the moments, of their delight, or great grief or even happiness.
To enter into a poet's mind, was indeed a privilege;
    To read their words from books of old
The stories that were never told, but we had to know the
    Truth and so we read, and tried to understand
All of their meanings, and all of their fears.

The poetry was timeless,
    But the maidens and the silvery brooks were far away,
And now the blue waters, dashing on the rocks
    Of Cornwall, on a windy day,
Brought back my memories of my summers spent
    On holidays, when we were young, and reading poems
I fell in love on a windy beach, on the southern bay.

A poem that I loved to read, and knew by heart
    It took me to another world, far, far away;
Where love was close at hand, and I could write my poem,
    And for eternity, young lovers could read my
Words to take them to another place, in poetry,
    Where our visions soar so high.
And the moments of this feeling will forever be set
    In a poem, so it will never be erased,
And a fleeting thought will never be forgotten,
    Of the poetry of a poem, with its ever-lasting sounds,
Of the murmur of the wind in the trees and
    The faintness of the waterfall and the beauty of
The clear mill pond.

A magical England, a magical place, with the old
    And the ancient castles on high.
The palaces and forts and the white cliffs of Dover
    Their poetry abounds, it speaks to us all,
As we make our way through the night and the day
    It speaks and makes us better men they say.
It softens the edges to create the art in our lives;
    As we wonder alone with a poet's book,
Our thoughts hold the poems dear;
    For the mysteries of life, we always look for,
Will remain just that, that we love, and are loved,
    But that man can shape his destiny;
But we do not know the future, and walking on
    Into the mists of time, we seek
To find ourselves, and by doing so, we are there.

What Is Love?

What is love, a question we all ask ourselves.
I think to question love is good, but we will
Never know the truth about love;
Love is so many things,
And for lovers, it is something that takes them
To a higher place, and a higher grace.
A transformation into oneness
That is experienced, but cannot be explained,
A oneness of thoughts and feelings
Of never wanting to part, of never wanting to say goodbye.

Love is a special warmth and connection with another human being,
It is the connection of ideas, and thoughts and laughs,
Love, is what we need to make us better people
To share, to give, and learn to be more than one's self.

Love means different things to different people,
But to have the warmth of an arm around one's shoulder,
And, yes, a shoulder to cry on, and feel better afterwards;
Love keeps us going through the best of times, and the worst of times.

To have the closeness and loyalty of a good friend
Is worth a lot in these busy modern times.
Together, going forward to work and live a full life,
A partner, and confidant, is what makes it all worthwhile.

To find love, to find a friend, we need to be warm,
And be ourselves, we need to laugh and enjoy our
Surrounds and to help one another; thus
By doing good deeds, we ourselves improve
And show that we can go forth, and help
To make this world a better place.

Love is a magnet to our hearts, it pulls us in
And doesn't want to let go;
To love, we must also see the other's point of view
And respect each other's wishes,
And together go forth always in the mist
Of preciousness and appreciation, that two people
Have found something special in each other,
And want to cherish the moment forever.

Student Days in London

The newness of the spring in London's parks,
With daffodils at every turn and ducks on ponds
And deck chairs sitting in the sun, with lovers kissing
their first sweet kiss.
Such memories when I was young and
School was really just for fun.

School days in London were such youthful fun,
I should have been studying hard.
What was the purpose of it all,
If one didn't fall in love? It was spring, after all
And daffodils were dancing in the sun, and
Dappled sunshine shone through the trees, in
London's parks where I loved to be free.

Then, there you were beside the lake in St James' Park
The willow tree, just like it used to be,
Where, in the snowy winter we did play,
Swinging out onto the frozen lake
Hoping the willow branch would not break.

Those days of tipping Bobbies' hats and
Running wild and free, just near
Buckingham Palace where we played, and then
Went back to school, where French was
Taught and manners too;
But I preferred geography on Friday afternoons.

I used to walk past Big Ben on my way to school,
And past Westminster Abbey where poets of
Another day, lay buried there for all to see,
The importance of their gift.
We learned their poems and now I see,
They helped me to write and to
Compose, my own poetry.

My favourite poet of them all, was Keats,
I think because he was a fragile man and sickly too,
He lay upon his couch and felt he had to write,
Because he had so much to say about the
Beauty of this world, and his sweetheart
That he would wed.

He wrote with her in mind,
He wrote because he did not have much time;
But he left behind his words and thoughts
And the beauty of his poems, which paint
A picture of the majesty of the deep forests
And glens and silvery streams, and nymphs
Dancing in joyous dreams.

I liked English Literature at school in Westminster
Where I fell in love with Keats;
His poetry took me to another world, a higher place,
And there I would always be, seeing life's
Beauty through his eyes, and would always realise
His poetry, was love in all its guise.

Then Big Ben chimed four o'clock
Which made it time for school to end;
And once again, I walked on past the grand buildings
Where England's laws are made.
It made me feel so serious, but at the same time
Delirious, for man makes the world go round
And poets write about the grand and grandeur of it all.

On thinking so many thoughts as I walk by
We achieve each day what we can, writing and
Learning, then every day we can say, that a
Poet's work is never done, another poem for
Another day, I suppose you could say,
In a very Parliamentary way, we're doing what we can.

Climate Change

How can this world, this planet of ours, be disintegrating in front of our
  eyes?
Is this due to mankind not caring, or is it something more than this?
Is it greed, is it war, is it famine and drought?
Yet I know that there is such diversity of thought,
When discussing how climate change came about.
There are many more issues concerning our world,
Be it greed and power, these are the worst of all,
For nations are caught up in their eventual fall,
From power and then to war.

The smaller countries with people suffering,
No water there at all.
The armies of the despots with their arms from larger
Powers, take on their own and slaughter them,
And when there are no people left
There is no country to support, no government, no help.
What happens next? Where do they go? These poor people
That are left will walk and walk to heavens knows where;
Their children sick and dying, on the way to no where
On the way from war.

These distant lands, where climate change has left its mark
Have nothing, no farms to grow food, no animals to eat.
There is no hope, the earth is dry, there are no clouds in the sky,
To make the rain to help the crops, to stop the wars,
And help the people back from the terrible abyss, before
Their world is no more.

What must we do, we ask ourselves, for we have more to give
But if we don't try to compromise, and realise that we who have more,
More water, more food, more rain, and good earth
To sew the crops, to give food to all the world;
To help in any way we can, to rescue people from the brink
To plant all the trees, to keep the planet from becoming extinct;
To look after the deep blue oceans and keep them clean from man's
Debris and excessiveness, of daily lives lived for comfort
And enjoyment, just tossed away on the high seas.

We have to keep the air around us pure and clean, we cannot
Let the temperature of our planet rise too high
Because we didn't care, or because we were too busy
And we thought it wouldn't matter, but the coal that is mined
And the fuel that we use is creating a caldron and causing
The climate to change around us, and the hurricanes are coming
Fast and furious, and damaging our towns and cities;
And in just one night of rage and flooding, all that was built has gone.

The flooding and the sun's deep heat, are causing our
Planet to be destroyed, and man and beast will not survive if
Our world is taken from us because we didn't pay
Attention to the scientists, who knew this time was coming,
With all the catastrophes in its wake,
Is it truly too late, to save our planet and our fate?

The Race

The mere wonder of being in a race, any race, is wonderment enough
To be a part of, to strive to do well, to enjoy the
Friendship of teammates, to help them too, is to be counted
As lucky, lucky to be there and good enough to take part.

What we must learn to understand, and learn, is
That we must just do our best, and if it isn't winning
Then enjoy the fact that doing one's best is winning.
It is the joy of the moment, we can be proud of.

We can take our moments and look back on them, one by one;
We can wonder if we could have done better,
We can feel the need to want this to last forever;
But it is now, that we benefit, from just a good race run.

We know our fans want to push us along to fame,
We know that we can't always be the same,
We try to please our fans along the way
But, we must stay true to who we are today.

Tomorrow, we may regret what we did today,
So we must win the race inside ourselves
The race that tells us we can win, but not at any cost.
We can win, if we are ready and we haven't lost.

We must not win at any cost, for any reason, or any thought,
Our egos are so very fragile, we want to be our best, and want to win,
But it isn't worth the cost, if we take the wrong turn, and abuse it,
For winning must be clean, and done on pure love and passion of the sport.

For it is at the end of the day, when we look back,
We will pay the price of having done things to enhance
The moments in the race to help us win,
But winning is from passion, and must be embraced,
To win is not everything, but to take part in a race
Is winning all the same.

We must feel good about our past, and look back on all our friendships,
To know, that deep in our hearts, we won the race and didn't cheat;
To think back and know the feeling that we took part in
Winning or losing with our team, these are the dreams
And moments that we will keep and cherish forever,
Knowing that we did our best, and now can feel complete.

Walks with My Love in France

Walks with my love in France were always an adventure,
And new paths we cut through the bracken,
Which would take us under trees and besides large rock-faced outcrops,
Standing on high, we could see all that lay beneath.

We strode along the shoulder of the mountain,
To reach the ridge along the top;
Falling away on either side was a nothingness, and we were
Flying and could not stop, along nature's paths, high in the
Cloudless blue of the Mediterranean sky.

Under the trees, and then suddenly we would find ourselves
Out in the sunshine, on the ridge, and looking over yonder at
Villages beneath, and looking all around, there were church
Spires that climbed the air, churches in every village square.

Colourful market towns, down below the mountain,
With grapes and wine and produce of a warmer clime.
Where bustling market day became a time to meet with friends,
And have a glass of wine, and languish for a little while
To take in the fragrance of the herbs, and fruit that lingered in the air.

As I think on these walks with my now-lost love, and
Recreate them in my mind,
I remember every detail and every path as we listened to the
Birds, and discovered the geology of the Earth
And old volcanos in the midst, with large rocks that spewed
Out of the earth, and the scree along the slopes and at the bottom of the cliff.

Yes, we were discovering all over again, the wonders of the
Silent forest and the glassy brooks with moss and dew,
A glen so quiet and yet so new,
We tiptoed through with quiet breath, not to disturb this
Peaceful dell, of woodland flowers and ferns,
And small waterfalls that fell.

Oh, such is my memory of my true love, with our oneness
And our dreams yet to come, but no more,
For my love is now in my dreams, through my walks and
Into the magic of the glen, we tiptoe through a special place
Where once we walked hand in hand,
A place we will always have,
Together, with my love in France.

Poem for Peace

People grieving all over the world
In so many countries, in so many ways,
Why has it come to this?

So many people, so many reasons,
The grief, the grieving, the tears of the world cascade over
Our consciousness and come to rest
In the souls of the departed.
The tears of the world won't extinguish these flames of hate, of terrorism, of
    fear.

We the people must rise up against this,
We must rise up, and be better than this,
We must rise up, and defend against this,
We the people, must help each other and
Help our villages, our cities and our countries,
Against the evil that is gradually inserting itself
Into our societies, into our schools, into our churches.

Our grief is everyone's grief, our sons and daughters are
Everyone's sons and daughters;
The guns, the slaughter, the murders, the hatred
Affect our sons and daughters of the world;
There is only one world, one chance, one life.

Let us awaken, at this time in our lives,
To undo the wrongs, to undo the ways that stop our progress
Into the visions we want to see, for our sons and daughters,
Around the world, in the villages, in the cities and in our hearts.

It is not too late, it is not too soon, it is not the wrong time
For this world to turn towards the light of enlightenment,
To turn towards all the best that human nature can aspire to.
To bring our knowledge to life, the knowledge that life is precious
The knowledge that life is not being wasted,
And bring all that is good, to work, to strive,
To find our very special place in this world.

Can our fractured societies start to work together,
Knowing that together, is better than never?
Can our Heads of State, our politicians, around the world
Realise now, that there is no time to waste?
Can the naysayers start to listen, start to realise, that
Without compromise, this world will not survive,
Will not be habitable, will not be possible, will not endure
Without the love, that humans share for each other;
Across boundaries, across countries, across oceans and across religions?

Without this love, there is nothing, there is turmoil and there is hate.
Let the leaders of this world come together, work together,
Strive together, to find the peace that the world needs,
And together, work towards repair, work towards strength,
Work towards unity of thought and deed,
So that mankind can take one giant step,
Once more, into greatness,
Love is all it takes.

The Castle of My Dreams

The castle of my dreams is atop the mountain yonder,
    Let us walk up there and discover the mystery of its walls;
Let us see and feel the hundreds of years of history that
    Cascade upon us,
As we find our way through the jungle of trees that now live
    Inside its walls.

As we scramble through the ruins, through the trees that
    Live there now
I can feel and hear those ancient people, dining in the great
    Hall
With candles lighting its majesty, where old pewter
    Chandeliers hung.
The grand oak table where the knights sat feasting, as the
    Wind howled outside,
And the logs burned bright in the huge fire place, it was
    Good to be inside.
I listen to them talking and I hear their secret words, as they
    Plot and plan amongst themselves
To go to war, to fight the clan, for war is so exciting and
    There are rewards,
More lands to conquer, more power to create and the ancient
    Family name at stake.

As we walk on down the mountain, I feel the history that we
    Left behind,
'Tis sad to see the castle in ruins now, it knew much better
    Days, yet savage too;
The wilderness of times gone by, now stretch before us to
    Wonder why,
But lingers on the edge of time, for wonderers to walk and
    Not forget.
So, through the trees we go, on the other side of wilderness,
    Where we walked;
A time gone by, but yet, is present in the mist.

The Big Old House

No, I never looked back as I walked through the courtyard
    To the gate at the street,
I could not look back at the sorrowful house
    Where my dear in-laws used to live.
Where we had such fun together, my husband and his
    Brothers, such summers were great
In the French countryside, when we paddled down rivers.

The big old house had known sorrow before,
    Before we were there;
But we knew joy too, when the Christmas tree
    Was bought, and stood in the hall.
We decorated it, with bright coloured balls,
    And put the star at the very top,
With the holly and ivy and added silver and gold thread;
    Such sparkle with the bright twinkly lights.
Not finished yet, we sprinkled white snow and cotton-wool tufts,
And finished in grand Christmas tradition,
    Raising our glasses of sherry, and savouring the hot mince pies.

Such fun in the kitchen, when cooking the turkey,
    All the family was milling around, some helping;
The wine was brought out and the good crystal glasses
    Good plates were laid, and crackers too.
It was fun to have all of the trimmings, it made the table grand.
The candles were lit and the table was ready;
    After all was enjoyed, with plenty of wine
To end it all, the great Christmas Pudding,
    With brandy alight in the dimmed candle haze,
All singing carols with gusto and fervour,
    A great Christmas dinner to always remember,
With family together, enjoying the season,
    In the big old house, on the Avenue de la Gare.

NOTES ON THE POEMS

NOTRE DAME DE PARIS

This is describing the feelings regarding the fire of Notre Dame and the deeper issues of what reactions we have to this and the love that everyone feels towards ND. Being that ND is the heart of Paris and loved by the world.

A POET'S MELANCHOLY

This poem describes how I would like to be able to write poems like poets such as Keats and Shelley and Wordsworth. But I know I can't. It describes how they have to suffer and feel pain to write about love. Painful love surrounds them and haunts them but they keep on writing. Perhaps they will find peace when they write about true love.

WHAT TIME IS IT?

This poem tries to find the time to discover time. Where does time go, how do we use time. Time cannot be harnessed, it must be used. Time seems like a mystery, where does time go. Time is never ending, we must try to seize the day.

A BEAUTIFUL WORLD TO SHARE WITH MY LOVE

A widow starts to write about her adventures with her husband and describes the beauty of nature, as their playground, kayaking, skiing, hiking. Friends around a campfire with the call of the coyote high up in the mountains. Out in the wilderness, under the stars, a beautiful world, to share with my love.

THE DAYS YOU LOVED ME

A sad poem, asking her husband not to forsake her just because his heart took a different turn. Not to turn away because she was whom he loved when he found her. The days of dancing and rivers and Texas were the days he loved her. Don't say goodbye just yet. This referred to her husband as he was dying, and she wanted him to think about the days he loved her.

UNDER THE BIG TEXAS SKY

The story of kayakers running rivers in Texas, and afterwards dancing in their field of dreams to Strauss waltzes under the Texas sky. And out of the blue a marriage proposal as they danced the night away, under the big Texas sky.

AN ODE TO A GENTLEMAN

A gentleman who loved music and playing the piano. He had his special tunes we all remember. His family and friends will remember him as playing the hymns in church and bringing their souls alive. He had a twinkle in his eye that kept him young and he would be always there to help if need be. He was a special person and each and every one will remember him because of his love of music and song.

GALLIPOLI

Gallipoli was the failure of command. The Anzacs landed at Gallipoli under heavy fire. There was no turning back, they fought their way up the beach and there were heavy losses. This is where the "mate-ship" started. They looked after each other under terrible circumstances. Mates looked after mates and today, we are a better nation because of this attitude. It still exists. It was a terrible war, but the Anzacs knew they had to win because humanity would never be the same if they lost. But the cost was huge on both sides. A terrible loss of life. Young boys left home to fight a most terrible war, they thought they were going to have a new adventure. Most of them were just young farmers. They did not know the ways of the world, let alone war.

THE NORFOLK FISHERMEN

The poem describes the hard life of the fishermen. Their love of the sea, even if they die at sea, they still love fishing. It's in their blood.

ENGLAND'S GREEN AND PLEASANT LAND

This poem describes the beauty of the English countryside. How it hasn't changed for many years. It is still as beautiful when Constable painted it many years ago. And how we need to keep it this way for our grandchildren to see and love.

LOVE IS THE REASON WE LIVE

A poem explaining that love is the reason we live. It brings hopes and dreams and pain. With the right attitude to loving and being loved, it is good for the world to have more love in it. Love makes us who we are for better or for worse.

POEMS AND OUR SOULS

The poets of yesteryear and their endeavours to write about beauty and love and sadness. We know by reading their poems that they left us their legacy. Their poetry opened our eyes to the beauty of how they expressed their love of beauty. Their poems will live on and we will benefit from having been taken on the magical rides through their mystical thoughts and phrases.

WHAT IS LOVE

This poem is about the mystery of love. How do we define it and how we find it. What are the ingredients of love and how do we preserve love. How love changes us and with love we become better people. It takes warmth, good deeds and helping one another and most of all respecting each other's views. And in the mist of love to appreciate the preciousness of love so that it may endure forever.

STUDENT DAYS IN LONDON

About student days in London. How freedom was important and also young love and the love of poetry. Spring in London's parks where daffodils were every-where and young lovers had their first kiss. The poetry of Keats was important in how it would mould a young girl's vision of the world. How walking past The Houses of Parliament and Westminster Abbey a student's thoughts became more serious, and thoughts were of the future and success.

CLIMATE CHANGE

Our planet is changing because of the higher temperatures. How climate change is causing wars, because of drought and famine and the greed of governments. The scientists who tell us about climate change must be listened to or we will not have a habitable planet for man or beast.

THE RACE

It's about a race, and how we should approach taking part in a race. How our passion for racing is pure and that whether we win or lose, we must not cheat. We have to be able to look back on our relationships with the team and ourselves and feel content. Winning is not everything; in fact, losing can be winning in itself. That at the end of the day, we must be able to look back on just being content that we were able just to take part. We must learn to be content with what we can achieve.

WALKS WITH MY LOVE IN FRANCE

Remembering the beauty of the walks in the mountains and the vistas and the green mossy glens where my love and I would walk under the Mediterranean sky.

POEM FOR PEACE

The people of this world must work together to procure peace for this world. So many people, sons and daughters are hurt by the inaction of politicians. If only we could come together and compromise and work towards peace so that mankind will have a future. One giant step once more into greatness. Love is all it takes.

THE CASTLE OF MY DREAMS

Upon coming across a castle on a mountain top. Thinking about the way the ancient people lived and fought wars for honour's sake and the family's name. Imagining the warmth of the fire and the pewter chandeliers in the great hall and the plotting and scheming of the warriors for their next war with the next clan.

THE BIG OLD HOUSE

The big old house has seen some sorrow in its day and also happiness. This tells the story of a happy Christmas enjoyed by a family. Decorating the Christmas tree and preparing the food in the kitchen with family all around. The wonderful celebration of the Christmas season with the whole family at the grand table, enjoying the wine and singing Christmas carols at the house on the Avenue de la Gare.